PÉTER KORNISS + ISTVÁN LÁZÁR

Hungary

PÉTER KORNISS ✦ ISTVÁN LÁZÁR

Hungary

OFFICINA NOVA · MAGYAR KÖNYVKLUB

WHERE IS HUNGARY SITUATED? Sometimes even this simple question is difficult to answer. Her latitude and longitude are easily defined. But what does that reveal? The geographical position of our small country today, its geological space – which, alone, expresses less than does Hungary's place in time. Where is Hungary situated? The geological record gives one answer. Plate tectonic experts say that, deep beneath the surface, the Carpathian basin is divided by a fault line – drawn on the surface by the volcanic range of the Hungarian mid-level mountains – along which a strip of the earth's crust that drifted here from the body of prehistoric Africa clasps onto prehistoric Eurasia. More recently – five or six thousand years ago, after humans appeared – *tells* sprang up in lines along the Tisza River, growing higher by the layers heaped up over the centuries. These dwelling hillocks are well known from Mesopotamia, Asia Minor and the Balkans, everywhere where the first impetus of the Neolithic era, the revolution of food production, had a direct effect. However, the westernmost and northernmost locations of the *tells* as they are called in Arabic – are with us, along the Tisza River. This is the frontier. This is where the spread of the New Stone Age development was blocked. That is, for a long time the cultural standard was much higher east of the Danube River than west of it. It was to be the opposite in all successive eras. Cultured East and barbaric West – that formula was never again to be repeated in Europe. So sometime around the birth of Christ, the Roman reign of the Latin era began, grew in strength for several centuries and finally collapsed in this region. The then-Roman *Pannonia provincia* corresponds more or less to today's Transdanubia. And its border, the *limes*, is the River Danube itself. This divides the well-organized Imperium from the dim Barbaricum here, in the heart of the Carpathian basin. The Hungarian people arrived here 1100 years ago along the long and bloody East-West path of the great migration. A thousand years ago, they settled in the Carpathian basin and founded a state. And when Latin Roman Christianity and Oriental Byzantine Christianity both offered themselves, the Hungarians chose the former. In this region, this is how the eastern edge of the Hungarian settlement area became a dividing line between the Gothics and the onion domes. Nor did the Protestantism that held sway over the Hungarians spread to the East from here. At the peak of its power, the Ottoman sultanate, expanding toward the heart of Europe, reached through the Balkans to the fringes of the Hungarian Great Plains and Transdanubia; it besieged, but could never seize, Vienna. The Leithe ("Lajta," in Hungarian) is a tiny river beneath Vienna and above the Fertő Lake – a lake divided by the Austro-Hungarian border. The Leithe is hard to find on maps. Still, the phrase "over the Leithe" became part of German consciousness when referring to the East. For this is the region, up to the Leithe, where the Germans (although called Austrians here) lived in a closed enclave; they came "over the Leithe" only sporadically, becoming a minority with the passing of time. It is already an irony of history that, in the middle of this century, as soon as the victory euphoria of World War II in 1945 evaporated and the Cold War loomed, the Iron Curtain divided Europe into two. The frontier between the western part, sentenced to a good life, and the eastern one, dominated by the Soviets, coincides with the Austro-Hungarian border – on the Leithe – which thus became a long-standing dividing line between the two world camps. Well, where is Hungary situated? She is also described as a "ferry country," drifting or desperately rowing between East and West. But whoever searches for her in Central Eastern Europe will fail to find her. For Hungary is situated in Eastern Central Europe. And this small shift in words carries a great meaning.

Transdanubia

A SMALL COUNTRY in itself. Its plain is the table-smooth Kis-Alföld (Small Plains), lying between rivers, full of water not long ago, thirsty only in recent times. Its range of hillocks embraces the Transdanubian Mid-level Mountains in a wide bend and its main body, the green Bakony hills. And Lake Balaton at its foot. From the west, its climate is cooled by the nearby Alps, which gives the area rain and, in wintertime, covers it with snow; in the south, Mediterranean mildness reaches the place from the Adriatic, and the summer heat of the Great Plains burns its eastern edge from the other bank of the Danube River. Its *epiteton ornansa*, or constant epithet, is gentle. Due perhaps to the soft, feminine forms of its hills? This is what poets believe. But the place enjoys a direct heritage from the remains of the Romans' almost five-hundred-year reign in Pannonia. This is believed not only by poets but also by the more prudent historians. But its spiritual climate is influenced most of all by its proximity to the West. People more quickly getting used to cities of stone, better adapting to their situation, more diligent, growing more familiar with civic virtues, used to live here. They were more affected by the Counter-Reformation and re-Catholicization. Large numbers of South Slavs and German speakers settled alongside the Hungarian population. Its forests are greater than its need for wood. It could sustain itself from its own food production. It has already consumed most of its mining resources. Its economy, however, is increasingly determined by its long-standing, reviving industry. This industry is now, in the final years of the twentieth century – although not for the first time – gaining a major impetus in this land. This prosperity allows the area's traditional cities – such as Sopron *(2)* – to maintain the buildings and traditions spared by the centuries.

GYŐR

This is how the paper *Életképek* (Genres) describes the topography of Győr, the capital of North Transdanubia, also referred to as the "Hungarian Ruhr" and, of course, as the Small Plains: "Győr spreads across a wide plain at the fork of the rivers Rába, Rábca and the Győr Danube. The downtown area lies in the southeast corner of the junction of the rivers, on the southern and eastern sides of which, the bastions demolished, a cheerful suburb has been built." As for the waters now, the "Győr Danube" is the Moson-Danube, or rather the Danube branch, whose water level has been fairly diminished since the commissioning of the Bős-Gabcikovo water barrage system in Bratislava, Slovakia. The river Marcal is also part of the river system of the city, which is why Győr is called the "city of four rivers." However, as for the bastions of the Püspökvár, also hiding an impressive labyrinth of casemates, its remnants still exist, precisely where the

3

4

Rába flows into the Moson-Danube *(7)*. And 150 years after *Életképek* described the town, the "cheerful suburb" can now be considered a historic relic itself, as a part of the old city of an increasingly flourishing, modern industrial center which, fortunately for the current age, cherishes many of the values of earlier centuries. Finally all Vienna-Budapest road traffic strangling Győr can now bypass the city. But those who visit the city for itself, for its atmosphere and historic assets *(5, 6)* or just to see the modern Győr Ballet, are still welcome.

PANNONHALMA

The well-known place of the Catholics of two peoples, the French and the Hungarians. In 316 or 317 A.D., a certain Márton was born here, in Sabaria of Pannonia. Later he became an imperial guard officer himself in Italy. Then he was elected the archbishop of Tours and finally became the patron saint of Gaul. He was the first saint who suffered no martyr's death. The Pannonhalma Benedictine abbey has a past of a thousand years, going back to 996. It was dedicated to Márton of Tours, just as the hill surrounded by the buildings of the abbey, which has grown every century since its existence *(9–12)*, also bears his name *(8)*. The renovated Pannonhalma Abbey, restored in the spirit of its millennial festivities, continues to operate. It teaches, protects and directs. Its library *(13)* holds, the Foundation Letter of the Tihany Abbey of 1055. Its knowledgeable priests have a major influence on modernizing the theological and spiritual life of Hungarian Catholicism today.

9

10

11

12

13

15

16

SOPRON

Under the name Opidum Scarbantia
Iulia, Plinius, the great Roman writer,
mentioned it as early as 15 A.D., so it
was a widely known town in the
Empire. However, of Hungary's
Roman-founded cities, this is the only
one whose ancient form has determined the present structure of the city
core. But only the ravages of bombing
in World War II brought to light to
what extent the fortress walls of the
late imperial era had been followed
and utilized in Sopron during the military construction works in the Middle
Ages. Thus the huge horseshoe or oval-
shaped place surrounded by a protective wall, where the population of the
late Pannonian times hid from the
barbarians ravaging the area, is reflect-
ed in the unearthed walls and the current street structure. Numerous other
medieval relics have been uncovered
(15). A planned town protection
seemed to exist in Sopron fairly early.
This town, built on the Ivy Path of
antiquity running from the northern
Baltics to the southern Mediterranean,

17

later prospered through trade as well. In the meantime, however, an increasing number of German speakers settled here. They carried civic virtues – love of the arts, art collection and serving the public in addition to enriching themselves – which made some of Sopron's aristocrat families famous. The exterior of the Storno house *(19–21)* not only cherishes the taste of this family but also houses a museum. A far view opens to the city, referred to also as the City of Loyalty, from the top of the Fire Tower *(18)*. The Trianon Peace Treaty closing World War I provided for Sopron to be annexed to Austria. Though the Sopron-area population indeed consisted of a slight majority of German speakers, they nevertheless contested the decision and got it annulled in a referendum.

20

19

21

KŐSZEG

It stretches at the foot of the Alps. The Austro-Hungarian border runs at the 882-meter-high Irottkő, a peak right above the city. Kőszeg's most memorable year was 1532, when Miklós Jurisich, the captain of Kőszeg's fortress, and a few hundred of his men withheld the Turks, besieging the West time and again since their victory at Mohács in 1526. He allowed his enemy to pin their war symbol with the pony-tail on the castle walls, but refused to surrender the fortress. As a result, the Sultan's 500,000-strong army lost power and time in the battle, and became unable to besiege Vienna. The Heroes' Gate was built 400 years later to commemorate this event *(24)*. Not only the bastions of the Jurisich castle, the Town Hall of Gothic origin *(23)*, the pharmacy museum and the count-less captivating details of the entire downtown area *(22)* attract one here, but also the sub-Alpine climate.

22

23

25

26

JÁK

Its recent past is marked by dedicated master potters living a semi-peasant life. Its distant past is represented by the church, where followers of the Catholic faith of Ják now go to mass and liturgy and where they give the oath "'till death do us part." *(25–26)* What could be more international in the Middle Ages than the Roman Church? Earlier, this three-nave, two-tower masterpiece of Romanesque architecture and sculpture was identified with Dalmatian masters; today its Italian and German style is mentioned instead. Its construction, which began in the 1210s, was halted by the Tartar devastation. Later the building suffered major damage by the Turks, primarily to the heads of its sculptures; the Islamic faith condemns such icons as "idolatry." But let's not forget the blaze that hit in 1567: the church was set on fire by Szombathely burghers, although the monastery was depopulated and the church deserted. Today it is one of Hungary's highly esteemed, precious historic relics.

27

SZOMBATHELY

The cult of Isis, the sister and wife of Osiris, the goddess of heaven and later the mother of every living creature, reached the northern provinces from Egypt via Rome, and long flourished in Savaria, the religious center of Pannonia, in the late imperial era. (Savaria was the Roman-era name of Szombathely. Its name was only one letter away from Sabaria, the Pannonhalma of Saint Márton of Tours.) In addition to the Isis sanctuary reconstructed from fragments, the still-usable section of the Ivy Path running from Scarbantia-Sopron to the south, covered with heavy stones, is a similarly spectacular Roman-era relic of Savaria-Szombathely.

VELEMÉR

Őrség. Göcsej. Hetés. The menfolk of these small regions in the southwestern edge of the country used to serve as border guards. And these peripheries are protected areas, with pristine nature, scattered archaic settlements, a traditional way of life and little-known historic relics. The late Romanesque church of Velemér – its blueprint Romanesque, the rest Gothic – was built in the late 1200s *(29)*. Its original wall paintings add to its value; we know more about them than just their age. A certain János Aquila, a master of Radkersburg, painted them in 1378. Unusually for the era, he depicted himself. He is clothed in a green coat and violet tights. His coat of arms serves as identification.

28

29

FERTŐD

Prince Miklós "Shining" Esterházy (1714–1790), field-marshal and diplomat, built a palace on old foundations in one of the small villages of his country-sized estates – then called Eszterháza, today Fertőd – surrounded by a grandiose park *(30–33)*, rivalling the palaces of Versailles and Schönbrunn. Was he generous? From his tremendous income, yes, in a prodigal way. And this aristocrat family could afford to employ Joseph Haydn as a court musician for three decades. In the meantime, the composer lived and composed in the Kismarton and Fertőd palaces of his masters. Most recently, Fertőd has been an agricultural research center; however, on occasions it continues to host musical events as well.

31

32

33

PÉCS

The orthodox Christian catacombs; the 900-year-old, four-tower cathedral *(34)*; rare relics preserved here after the long Turkish rule; the djami and minaret of Jakovai Hassan *(36)* and the downtown parish church that also used to be Gazi Kasim pasha's djami *(37)*; the Zsolnay ceramics factory and the Zsolnay well *(35)* make Pécs the capital of the "Hungarian Mediterranean," close to the Adriatic Sea.

35

36

37

38

39

PÉCSVÁRAD

The mosaic Calvary of Pécsvárad *(38)*, a Mecsek village rich in historic relics beneath a canopy of branches.

VILLÁNYKÖVESD

Rivalling Sopron and Eger, Villány is the third of Hungary's wine regions famed for its excellent, fiery red wines. The row of cellars is a beautiful sight, even to the sober *(39)*.

40

MOHÁCS

The "cemetery of our national greatness," the site of a fateful battle lost against the Ottoman army in 1526 at Mohács. Many legends about the Turks live on here. For example, the *busó* procession *(40–41)*, this noisy and colorful pageant with frightening masks. Cannon and fire is considered by the Mohács inhabitants and by the Sokác people (a small South Slav people) as the revival and commemoration of a trick that once deterred the Turks. However, this annual folk festival is also known in other regions as a disguised burial of the winter.

41

PAKS

The raw material mine of the Paks brick factory exposes to geological and climate researchers the 50-meter-thick, richly layered cross-section of loess moldered from frost-bitten stones, dried by the sun and grabbed, carried and heaped up by the winds of the Ice Age and the following milder periods of 700,000 years. What is uncovered to us by this geological cross-section with its collectable pollen, the bones of tiny creatures and other findings is the ancient past of the strip of eastern Transdanubia richly covered by loess elsewhere as well. Then the settlement of Paks – to take a huge step in time – became famous for gastronomy, for the

"*halászlé*," the carefully guarded recipe of the Paks version of the ubiquitous thick fish soup, also prepared, cooked and spiced in many places along the rivers Danube and Tisza, a bit differently in each place. And as the Danube made Paks a fishermen's settlement, the town owes its newest turn of fate to this river as well. From there its water helps cool Hungary's only nuclear-power plant, built here after a long search for a site. With the nuclear energy-producing equipment of Paks, supplying four-tenths of the country's entire electricity needs, a highly advanced technology settled here. The main building, the power plant and the adjoining edifices, dramatically changed the traditional

landscape and structure of the gentle loess area along the river. The new Catholic church *(42–43)* built in this rigid industrial landscape between 1987 and 1991 gains special significance; its architect dips into the depth of past. Imre Makovecz – and a group of his followers, already considered a school – intended to drive Man back to the World Spirit, to gods – by the passionately applied wood,

and primarily by the organic forms, the almost living creature-like or totemistic finish of the buildings – to his more natural life medium and to the warmth of his small communities. Their style includes yurt forms, edgy towers, feminine arches. And big, ecstatic and inviting eyes; similar ones adorn the entrance of the Evangelic church *(44)* built in Siófok.

45

46

ZIRC

In the heart of "Bakonyország" (Bakony Land), Zirc is the first town in Hungary to be covered by snow in wintertime. The Cistercian abbey was founded in 1182. Prince Saint Imre's sculpture stands on the columns of the destroyed old church today. The new abbey church and building is a Baroque masterpiece; the library's reading hall and collection are unique. There is an arboretum behind it *(45–48)*.

TATA

Mining, by tapping the karst water system, did not rob the waters of the mill and the moat, the Öreg (Old) and Cseke lakes, but those of the once so-enchanting Fényes sources. Perhaps not for good. The Esterházy counts transformed the Öregvár of Tata *(48)*, surrounded by a lake and a moat, to make it look more historic.

47

The Danube Bend

O N ITS LONG, SNAKING path from the Black Forest of the German Medium Mountains to the Black Sea, the Danube River slowed first beneath Vienna, on the Small Plains, then spread widely, to break into branches containing large islands. But soon the river was again squeezed between mountains and was able to roll on again comfortably after skirting the forested block of the Pilis hills, turning sharply south, at the western fringe of the Great Plains. When the Magyars conquered the entire Carpathian basin 1100 years ago, including Transdanubian Pannonia, taking a thorough look there, precisely 1000 years ago, upon the state foundation, the establishment of the Hungarian kingdom, they marked out the axis of rule along the line from Székesfehérvár, then protected and surrounded by an extensive marshland (long a coronation and royal burial place), to Esztergom *(49)*, with the huge Pilis forests in the vicinity providing ample shelter. And from Esztergom, from the upper mouth of the Danube Bend, the center of Hungarian kingdom and the supreme royal residence itself were transferred to Buda, just under the bottom of the big bend along the Danube – only later. The little arable land in the area covers a big island curving along with the Danube from Visegrád to Szentendre. Thus the river was escorted on both banks by an almost unbroken ribbon of orchards, squeezed between the forests of flood areas and mountains. This zone is now increasingly developed. And the smaller and bigger settlements of the Danube Bend, with holiday cottages and permanent dwellers alike, line up closely. From Budapest to Visegrád on the right bank of the Danube and from Budapest to Vác on the left, a chain of holiday settlements appears in this beautiful landscape.

50

52

51

VISEGRÁD

The citadel was built after the Tartar devastation between 1250 and 1258, under the reign of Béla IV, as a shelter for the queen in the event of a disaster *(53)*. Massive construction work began around 1320 close to the foot of the hill, on the narrow Danube embankment. It was hard to believe the enthusiastic description by Archbishop Miklós Oláh of Esztergom – from the recent past – on the palace *(50–52)* housing innumerable halls and hanging gardens, offering – so to say – white and red wine from its marble wells on special holidays, built, then repeatedly rebuilt and adorned. But this century's excavations proved the archbishop at least partly right. Up in the citadel, the most valuable treasure of the independent Hungarian state, the royal crown, was safeguarded for two centuries – and so was the Polish crown, for a time, during the Hungarian-Polish personal union of Louis the Great. The greatest event in the history of the riverfront palace was the Visegrád royal meeting in 1335. Then King Charles Robert (Károly Róbert) of Hungary, King John (János) of the Czech kingdom, King Kazimierz (Kázmér) of Poland, Count Charles of Moravia, Bavarian and Saxon princes as well as the German Order of Knights – with an anti-Habsburg edge and after several months of negotiations – concluded an economic and political agreement that promised an early European common market. If it had been observed...

54

55

ESZTERGOM

Prince Géza – inviting priests and bringing a Bavarian princess as wife for his son Stephen – made a wise decision to found a state, and it was then fulfilled by King Stephen I, or Saint Stephen. It was Géza who built a palace on top of the Esztergom hill. Later, when the Roman Catholic church establishment was set up, the prince-primate and the *homo regius* – at the top of the hierarchy in later centuries – were placed here, authorized to crown the king or even replace him in case of need. It was the center of Hungary at the time. The outstanding church and national role that Esztergom thus gained greatly increased when it ceased to be a royal seat. And although the archbishop of Esztergom had a

palace in the Buda royal castle for a long time, its name was only recently changed to Esztergom-Budapest archbishopric. This is how Esztergom remained basically a priests' town. The Classicist basilica was built on ruins in the last century; the Esztergom Cathedral *(57)* rules the townscape as well as the Danube river flowing on the opposite side, at the foot of the hill. Its monumental cupola *(55)* generates perhaps more respect than piety. The Renaissance chapel of the pope-designate archbishop Tamás Bakócz, the royal chapel built by Burgundy masters in the 1200s *(54)*, and the Treasury of the Cathedral and the Christian Museum in the archbishop's palace beneath the castle hill sit.

56

57

35

58

SZENTENDRE

The geometry of the sloping and bending streets *(59)* of the old polygonal squares and the closely fitted houses and roofs in random order have attracted and inspired generations of painters. The reshapers of the town's folklore and faith were the South Slavs, who came up here from the Balkans to escape from the Turks. Therefore, one can see a variety of Catholic *(60)* and "Serbian" *(61)* churches; however, their clocks, if they work, show identical times. Not easy times at all. Of course, in the settlement that once fit snugly between the southeastern foot of the Pilis mountains and the Szentendre branch of the Danube river, the Nostalgia Court *(58)* may offer a taste of olden times. But despite attempts to preserve traditions and values, the town has almost been torn to pieces thanks to its proximity to Budapest and its own beauty. The overwhelming numbers of guests in the summertime are almost depressing. And the traffic of the whole Danube Bend flows through the town.

59

60

61

62

The Balaton area

NEVER HAS THERE BEEN a more lively death. Sadly, Central Europe's largest lake – its age is in the millions! – has long shared the fate of decaying old age in a geological and hydrological sense. But enduring so much, still, how attractive it is, what a stormy life it always had... In that fairly hollow, Pleistocene-age dip, now cradling 600 square kilometers of water glittering in the sunshine, Lake Balaton was once twice as big. The Romans, who called it *Locus Pelso*, liked it very much. They concentrated in the mild-climate area and put a sluice on the lake's bottom end. Did they want to drain it off? Or just to regulate its water a bit to fix its shoreline, as is done nowadays with the help of the Sió channel? It was later suggested, several times, that the lake be fully drained. Fortunately, this never happened. Even so, the lake was deprived of a bay, an arm with rich fauna and flora, as a consequence of natural filling up and of the organic waste of irresponsible man. The lake is shallow. The average water depth is three meters, and only 11.5 meters even in the "well", beneath the Tihany peninsula *(63)*, which is crowned by an abbey church. This is why the lake's water quickly warms to such a pleasant temperature. But it also cools down quickly as the winds blowing down from the Bakony hills during summer storms break the water's mirror surface into high waves. The lake is tightly ringed by an almost unbroken, built-in holiday zone. The north shore of the Balaton is not only a gallery of exceptional geological forms but also a high-quality wine region. But the curative mineral and thermal waters springing in abundance in the area are esteemed as well. All in all, Lake Balaton, inviting and offering, gives livelihood to many and recreation to countless others. Beauty and richness radiate from it.

64

It was my father – who grew up in Zala and lived in Zemplén – who told me that Hungary's two most beautiful views are found in the south, the Bada-csony silhouette viewed from in front, from the Zala-Somogy, i.e. southern shore of Lake Balaton *(64)*, and up in the north, the arch of the Zemplén hills over Sárospatak viewed from the Bodrogköz. Of course, this might also be a matter of taste. So it is better to insist on facts. On the southern shore of Lake Balaton, the water is shallower and one can walk farther into it *(67)*; silky sand covers the lake bed. In front, on the northern shore, one reaches deep water after a few steps, and in some places – mostly in the Keszthely bay – a thick layer of mud has settled. Reeds were once more abundant *(65)* – they are not only pleasant to the eye,

65

66

67

68

but also useful in keeping the water clean. No sport-boats are allowed to disturb the water of the lake, this huge bathing basin; sailors and surfers are all the more welcome here *(66, 68)*. Fishers battling the elements in storms *(70)* and their equipment on quiet water *(71)* and anglers favoring the quiet of their shelters share the lake's fish *(69)*, even if not always in idyllic peace. Fishers, who once had an almost exclusive rule over the lake, or

69

at least over its profit, supplement their fish money with ice cutting and reed harvesting in wintertime. Anglers often spend more on their quiet passion than the value of the fish they catch. The Balaton provides entertainment, existence and life itself for many. And the latter are those who take better care of its ecology than its economy. May a bright golden bridge span for them to the future, to the lake's future, however old it may be.

70

71

72

75

KESZTHELY

Close to the mouth of the Zala river, the only water source feeding the lake with its small volume of water, and to the carefully protected marshland of the Small Balaton – once almost dried out but now on the way to recovery – Keszthely is a quite urban small town around Lake Balaton which has not suddenly swelled up from a village to a town but developed organically through the centuries. The nearby excavations in Fenékpuszta lead back to antiquity, and it is possible that Theodoric the Great, king of the Goths, was born here. The splendid palace of the Festetics family (who spent a great deal on the cultural and public life at the turn of the 1700s and 1800s in the era of Prince György but later turned toward an egocentric, aristocratic way of life) became a museum *(74–75)*; game hunting is one of the main focuses of its rich library.

TIHANY

The foundation letter of its abbey and its crypt, which also serves as a royal burial place, originate from the 11th century. For centuries, it had been a poor fisher's settlement separated from the world. Today it is an exclusive holiday resort *(63)*. It connects its past, present and future by protecting the hermitages in the lime tufa caves, the inner lake – branch-Balaton – of the peninsula, the sights of handicrafts and the historic treasures of the local folk architecture.

76

77

78

79

BALATONUDVARI

When one can bathe, sunbathe and fly on the wing of winds filling the sails, the water, the lake are the main attractions. On the cooler, more cloudy days, however, many set out to discover adventures around Lake Balaton. This is how one can find, among others, the Balatonszentgyörgy Csillagvár (Star Castle) of 1820 built in an archaic style, the water-mill in Örvényes, the geyser cones of Tihany, the "bread field" attacked by volcanoes near Kővágóőrs, the Szigliget Castle, the volcanic cones of the Tapolca basin, the basalt organs in Badacsony and many others; including the heart-shaped Baroque folk tombstones of the tiny Balatonudvari cemetery. Heart-shaped tombstones? A beautiful way to cherish the long-standing memory of those passed away, in the hearts of the living.

80

NAGYVÁZSONY

Whoever starts from around Balatonakali, the middle of Lake Balaton's northern shoreline, either toward Budapest or Vienna, is advised to make his way northward through the colorful mosaic of the north shore of the Balaton reaching the road between Veszprém and Tapolca, to stop a bit at the Nagyvázsony castle *(78)*. Although only its residential tower remained relatively intact, it is one of those ancient castles serving as its masters' fortress and dwelling place. Nagyvázsony, providing historic sights in addition to the Kinizsi castle, is the venue of popular equestrian games *(79)*, evoking the medieval knightly tournaments.

TÁC

Gorsium, the Roman town, is situated not beneath Tác, the village of today, but in the immediate area. This made it possible to unearth and display Pannonia's sacral center. The extensive and spectacular ruin of Gorsium is guarded by a matron: the tomb of Flavia Usiau in a Celtic-Eraviscus outfit. The deceased is taken to the other world by a two-horse coach; a coachman stands on the driver's seat with two servants behind him.

VESZPRÉM

Hungary has only a few towns as split up by natural formations as Veszprém, which is divided by the Séd brook, squeezed in the canyon and built on five hills. It is duly represented by the bird's-eye view of the Castle Hill (82) studded with archaeological and historic relics.
The Episcopal palace in the classicizing late Baroque style (rebuilt several times, always in different styles but finally re-Romanticized), the Episcopal cathedral, the Trinity column and the Franciscan church stand in its axis.

81

82

47

83

SZÉKESFEHÉRVÁR

The center of the same region and economic zone whose heart was once Gorsium. Medieval Alba Regia, later Székesfehérvár, was partly constructed from the stones carried here from its predecessor of the Antiquities. Still, it is also the savior of Gorsium – it did not settle among and onto its walls but rather onto several islands of the marshland then considered more defensible. So it now stands on its own ruins from its earlier eras. Only the foundations of its first, four-section Carolingian – or Caucasian? – church have been recovered. Perhaps this church was pictured on one side of King Stephen's first denaria (which soon became an international-standard value setter). Also, the basilica, founded in 1016 in Stephen's era, was almost completely destroyed; for five hundred years, a coronation church and royal burial place where 37 Hungarian kings became legitimate rulers by the coronation ceremony and 17 kings were buried. In part, the Episcopal palace built in 1800-1801 in the Zopf style of the 16th century was placed on its foundation walls with the stylistic statue of the country apple, one of the coronation regalia, in front *(84)*. Whichever way one takes to the downtown section, one finds noteworthy sights: churches and sculptures *(85)*, town sections and buildings *(83, 87)*. One is the town hall put together from two buildings, one half of which – a one-story house also built in the Zopf style – served the same purpose back in 1689. The sculpture of Justice and Peace stands on the two sides of its balcony above the main entrance *(86)*. Accidentally, during World

84

War II, Justice was destroyed and so was carved again, with slight, deliberate differences, as if to acknowledge the loss of the old one. Although not a rarity elsewhere, the nicely fit, overhanging closed balconies *(87)* are traditional in this

86

85

town. Székesfehérvár grew spectacularly between the two world wars as well, especially concerning the sites related to the year 1938, the 900th anniversary of the death of King Saint Stephen. Its overall style is marked by the Neo-classicist "Roman school" of Hungarian painters, sculptures and architects. Thus the nude male on Pál Pátzay's famous equestrian sculpture ordered as a Hungarian hussar's monument instead seems much more like a Greek-Roman athlete who happens to be holding a medieval sword. Vilmos Aba Novák's fresco in the Saint Stephen mausoleum was whitewashed after 1945 – not because of its style but because of some of the side-figures on the historical tableau. It should also be mentioned that some old plants of the area's long-cherished, then crisis-ridden industry have been revived and new "greenfield" ones settled here by foreign investors, and this prosperity already not hoped for, is nevertheless promising for all Fehérvár. Perhaps it will be able to afford continued and better protection of its assets.

87

The Northern Mountains

*T*HE BÖRZSÖNY, CSERHÁT, MÁTRA, BÜKK AND ZEMPLÉN (or Tokaj) mountains range from the Danube Bend toward the east-northeast in a chain. A chain together. Separately they wear both similar and different faces. Similarities and differences in the landscape, in people's existence and in their lives. Don't expect soaring peaks. The highest, the Mátra, barely exceeds a thousand meters above sea level: the Kékes peak is 1015 meters tall. More characteristic are the 500–600-meter peaks, relatively high for Hungary. The highest and best-known are surrounded by their more modest counterparts, as aristocrats are surrounded by their feudal escorts. As if all these members of the northern mountains were banderia and were marching along the edge of the plains in a military or ceremonial order. The plebeian Alföld admires them from beneath. It is, however, the other way round. Most of the population of the northern mountain range lived this way for centuries: in the summers they earned their living down there, in more fertile regions; many went back to their home villages only in the wintertime. Some live this way today. Of course, there used to be wood cutting, timber-work, lime and charcoal burning; in older times there were glass-works and pearlash cooking. And there used to be mines, some of them still operational. But the shafts, courts and pitheaps of most of them have become idle and will grow no longer; the earth's wounds have stopped deepening. Work in them has died away. The old and now-deserted ore mines of the Börzsöny, Mátra and Zemplén hills, but also a number of stone mines, have become famous for the "mine flowers," the crystal miracles fantastically rich in color and shape, for the pleasure of mineralogists and avid minerophiles.

90

EGER

Hungary's collective memory has preserved the first
Turkish siege of 1552, which we considered so glorious.
Commander István Dobó and his two thousand soldiers
repelled the hundred-thousand-strong Ottoman army for
five weeks and forced them to withdraw, while the resi-
dents escaped to the castle. The event is depicted in
Hungarian writer Géza Gárdonyi's novel "Stars of Eger,"
written in 1901. This might be why more care and expense
has been devoted to the renovation of the Eger castle than
to that of most other Hungarian castles *(89–91)*. Eger's
second siege in 1596 was less memorable. This time the
defenders – now foreign mercenaries – put up no resistance
Eger was Turkish for 91 years afterwards. A minaret was
quickly built in the town *(89)*, from which the muezzin
professed Allah's glory until 1687. Legend holds that the
history or at least the christening of Eger's famous wine,
known the world over, also goes back to the period when
the Prophet Mohammed's laws ruled the town. Accordingly,
the excellent red wine gained the name "bikavér" (bull's
blood), so the followers of the true faith could pretend that
what they drank was not a prohibited alcoholic drink.
Otherwise, bull's blood is not the product of the grape with
the same name, but is the result of mixing "kadarka,"
"nagyburgundi" and "medoc noir," with some "oporto" and
"cabernet" added to it. Here in Hungary, pure medoc is pre-
ferred. Like so many towns in Hungary, downtown Eger's
face is dominated by the Baroque style of the post-Turkish
era and by Classicism spreading later. In the meantime,

91

Eger's burgher's houses *(94)* were built of stones carved from the depth of their own cellars, undermining the town by channels, just as in Pécs, Szekszárd and Szentendre, frequently causing cellars to collapse. Finally, let's quote a description of Eger's basilica, the Episcopal cathedral *(92)*, built in the Classicist style in 1837, upon its consecration: "Two sections of stairs lead to the majestic church hall; right from the start, one encounters two holy kings of our country, and one can see two major heroes of the mother church, Saint Peter and Saint Paul at the second. All these and the rest of the church's sculptures were sculpted by the well-known Venetian master, Marco Casagrande. Leaving these behind, one finds oneself in the hall with the most beautiful proportions, resting on eight Corinthian columns..."

93

94

55

95

Hollókő

It is very difficult to be part of the world heritage. The honor carries as many conditions and obligations as it does advantages and admiration. The World Heritage Convention came to life in Paris in 1972 under the auspices of UNESCO, the United Nations Educational, Scientific and Cultural Organization – a world heritage convention whose list currently includes about a thousand sites. From Hungary, which acceded to the convention only in 1985, first the Buda Castle District and the adjoining panorama of both quays of the

96

Danube river's downtown section, as well as Hollókő and the surrounding area, won this honorable but burdensome attention, joined later by the karstic region of Aggtelek; an inner section of a capital formed by centuries, whose development can be slowed, but never stopped, never frozen; an almost museum-like but still populated old village with rich ethnographical diversity, and a natural treasure, a geological zone with caves and other geological and hydrological formations. Hollókő is a tiny settlement in Nógrád County with a burdensome destiny. It is one of Hungary's mountain villages with a single, winding road taking one there and back, but not further. Nothing made its small castle famous. Until the researchers of peasant life and architecture discovered the unspoiled landscape *(96, 98)* and the love of tradition evinced by its devout Catholic villagers *(95)*, even its name was hardly pronounced elsewhere; it had been hidden in its shelter unnoticed.

97

98

99

101

100

RIMÓC

The Lord's Day – the holiday of the Holy Communion – in Rimóc. "Their blood is mixed with the blood of soft-speaking Slavs, and the landscape around them is the home of the charming rather than that of the splendid. Above the gloomy and simple black-and-white world of the Alföld people, they are the color: even their eyes are different from those down below. Those above have a sharp look, narrowing their eyes in some way, looking far into the distance, while those below look closer, have an eye for soft curves; their movement is faster and wittier and their talk is full of sweet flavor. Those down below shake the naked walls of the Protestant church by psalms, and their prayer is almost threatening, as they pray to Mary's son in prolonged, slow songs.
The believers in the hills live not far from them and the trunk of short trees grin on lost children at night. This landscape invites mystery. Not the desperate, bitter and dark mystery which is a veil on the life of sectarians, but a milder, more religious and more satisfied mystery. For them, what religion allows is sufficient for food, and spice is what superstition allows them to suspect," writes Zoltán Szabó, a writer/village researcher, in his book *Cifra nyomorúság* (Fancy Poverty) about those in the Rimóc area. The landscape of their village near Hollókő is not so intact, and so the people insisted all the more strongly on some of their cultic traditions, such as a cult of the deceased, the cemetery near the church and visits of the family tombs for a few minutes after masses.

102

103

MISKOLC

Hungary's second largest town beneath the bell-tower of its church on the Avas hill *(103)* and the TV tower so unbecomingly rising above? Only in the past. The development of Miskolc, an industrial city in the eastern gate of the once-proud Bükk hill, has been broken. This, however, only increases the value of Görömböly-Tapolca with its thermal water, Diósgyőr with its castle and other long-standing natural and historic assets of the Bükkalja area.

SZÉCSÉNY

Behind an ornamented fence: the Baroque Forgách palace *(104)*, built onto the old castle. Beneath it, Ferenc Rákóczi II, then Prince of Transylvania, convened parliament in the autumn of 1705 on the Burjúpást meadow.
A novel sight of the historic small town is the Baroque fire tower, which leans a bit as a result of bombing in 1944. Unlike the famed Leaning Tower of Pisa, however, it stopped falling.

104

105

LILLAFÜRED

The dam of its swollen Hámori lake *(105)* in the valley mouth of the Garad-na brook was constructed back in the 1810s. Its palace hotel *(106)* never served as a palace. It was built between 1927 and 1930 as a luxury hotel. Later, even as a trade-union holiday home, it tried to maintain its uniqueness. Many times, in both periods, it served as a backdrop for films. On such occasions it looked fairly artificial. Although it is fairly genuine, as it were...

106

SZILVÁSVÁRAD

The Bükk hill is full of surprises on its fringes and in its heart as well. The Bükk National Park does not seek to prohibit but only to regulate visits there. There are certainly pristine, undiscovered parts in the caves of the area. Its trout-filled waters in the Szalajka valley are the laboratories for fish farms as well. Viewed from a distance, the Szilvásvárad stud seems free here. One can observe the rough trunk fence only from a closer distance.

107

DIÓSGYŐR

It first belonged to national potentates, then was the favored castle of Anjou Louis the Great (1342–1382), became the venue of far-reaching diplomatic events of the Hungarian-Polish personal union and was then held by queens. It became a place for relaxation and the starting point of splendid hunting sessions organized by the royal court in the Bükk hill *(108)*. Relatively distant from the major marching paths of armies, it quickly lost military significance. Its unearthing, restoration and preservation has been exemplary. The settlement beneath the castle, increasingly merging with Miskolc, has become a bastion of heavy industry – the source of its misfortune today.

TOKAJ-HEGYALJA

A string of the most appropriate places for producing the "king of the wines" and "wine of the kings" ranges saw-toothed in a narrow stripe between the Bodrog river *(110)* and the Zemplén hills. Tokaj-Hegyalja's northern boundary is undisputed. That may be only at Sátoraljaújhely, tucked beneath the Sátoros hills. The lower, southern border is less certain around Szerencs and Mád *(109)*, under Tállya. The best wines in the region are promised by the slopes and vineyards of Ujhely, Patak, Tolcsva, Erdőbénye, Tarcal, Tokaj, Mád and Tállya, varying every year. And although the genuine, noble Tokay wine – "furmint," "hárslevelű," sweet and dry "szamorodni" and mostly the "aszu" varieties –

108

109

110

63

111

112

113

requires the strict observance of old, painstaking traditions, life goes on, of course. This is evidenced by the eye-catching new houses of Tolcsva at the end of the cordon-cultivated vineyard rows *(113)* and the tractors taking over the hoeing between the rows of the Tarcal field *(114)*. Do I seem biased? Well, I was born there: in the queen of this region, the "Athens of the Bodrog shore," Sárospatak, with the one-time queen's castle, and the esteemed Reformed college. In the pictures: the woodcarvings of the Renaissance triple window of the Perényi wing of the Rákóczi castle's palace section *(115)*; the balcony of Princess Zsuzsanna Lórántffy *(116)* on the western facade of the Lórántffy wing *(117)* and the knotted Pharmacy house *(119)* with the butterfly windows from the main street.

114

115

116

117

BOLDOGKŐVÁRALJA

Looking from the south – is that a brave eyrie on the peak protruding high? The view is a bit deceptive. If we make our way from the north, the "siege" is somewhat less tiring, to reach the top of this fortress *(118)* of the Hernád valley, on the brink of the Zemplén hill, known as early as the late 1200s. To take a look down to the tiny village, whose location is so easily found: right beneath Boldogkő castle. Somewhat higher, in the upper Hernád valley: the Kéked palace from King Matthias's era, the Hussite house in Gönc, the Gothic churches of Vilmány and Korlát, the former Episcopal palace in Hejce and the Regéc castle.

118

119

The Alföld (Great Plains)

*H*OW MUCH ITS GEOMETRY has changed in this century! Farmsteads have disappeared, leaving patches of shrubs for a while, then only a slight coloring of the soil. Half a century ago, the huge Alföld fields were cut up by the land reform of the time, then its small plots were plowed together again by the tractors of state farms, to be divided up yet again, until economic interests changed the situation again. But in the meantime the area of villages and towns doubled: a swatch of forest was grown here, another cut there; the water of fishponds and rice fields glitters here and there, and only mud remained elsewhere. But any change in the Alföld depends on water, although even the first centuries of this millennium have left their traces: the fewer forests, the free wind and cultivation have changed the face of the Alföld tremendously since the Magyar Conquest. River regulation and flood protection in the past century put an end to the floods, in which, several times a year, the Tisza and its adjacent waters turned into seas, making the place accessible only by boat or mud-ship; one had to flee from the area. But the usefulness of a safer life and the increased plow-land is greatly reduced by the drying out of the Alföld – perhaps witnessing a slow change in climate? – and the droughts, which recently have become almost annual events. Even so, this big field is a huge horn of plenty. It produces durum wheat, "édes-nemes" paprika, special-flavored fruit and vegetables and herbs full of flavor. This is how we boast of ourselves. It is all thanks to the peculiar soil and climatic endowments of the Carpathian basin. Some foreign tradesmen and customers have already discovered it – but not many. Our Great Plain is more famous abroad for its many natural beauties.

121

122

KECSKEMÉT

It is also called agro-Hungary or – no pejorative intended – the capital of peasant Hungary. The title is not for its size, but for the fact that it is one with Hungarian agriculture. This is probably due to its processing industry, which is affected by every trend in Hungarian agriculture. This settlement also demonstrates how agricultural development – taming the sand here into arable land – has a town-building and developing effect. In its willingness to act as a patron at the end of the last century, Kecskemét was a major supporter of Hungarian Secession greatly influencing the Alföld's landscape. In addition to the most frequently mentioned Town Hall designed by the architect Ödön Lechner, the richly adorned masterpiece of this style is the Cifra Palace (Fancy Palace) *(121)*; long a trade union headquarters, now housing the Kecskemét Gallery. The Kodály Memorial by the sculptor Miklós Melocco *(122)* reveals the function of the building towering behind it: it houses the model school bearing the Master's name, keeping alive and spreading the singing and music-teaching method developed by the composer Zoltán Kodály. Nine-tenths of Hungary's rural Jewry perished in the Holocaust. Kecskemét remained without a significant Jewish community. Its synagogue, built in 1862, carefully and faithfully restored, now serves as the town's House of Science and Technology *(123)*. Its purposes include the presentation of the collection of the Museum of Hungarian Naive Artists and the foundation, maintenance and enriching of the toy museum, the Szórakaténusz Playhouse, which collects, presents and revives children's folk games as a labor of love.

123

SZEGED

Studying the town's maps, one notices the name of the widely arcing outer boulevard's sections built according to the principles of French town designer G. E. Haussmann (the transformer of Paris). Town and capital city names are seen there. Szeged was washed away by a flood on March 12, 1879. The ice blocking the bed of the Tisza River melted and poured so much water onto thc town that barcly 300 of its 5,600 houses were still inhabitable. It was a major catastrophe attracting world attention. Reconstruction took only four years, and the grateful citizens of Szeged immortalized the names of the cities abroad that provided the largest volume of aid. Later, competing for the rank of the country's second largest town, Szeged spent a great deal on enriching itself with cultural and scientific institutions.

125

126

127

128

The museum named after the writer and archaeologist Ferenc Móra and the building of the Somogyi Library bearing the name of the donor, Károly Somogyi, the canon of Esztergom *(126)*, bear witness to this, as does the city's long battle for a university of its own. Szeged was one of the sites where Albert Szent-Györgyi conducted research on Vitamin C, work for which he won the Nobel Prize – the only Hungarian so honored while still living in Hungary. World War I disrupted the building of Szeged's Eclectic cathedral, mixing several new styles *(125)* and finished only in 1930. In the summer Dóm (Cathedral) tér is the venue for plays and musical pieces requiring monumental productions. The noted personalities of Szeged to whom the town erected statues include the Gypsy songwriter Pista Dankó, who could not even read music *(128)*. The Tisza River, actually over-regulated and squeezed between dams, sometimes still dangerous, dividing the city into Old and New Szeged, adds greatly to the town's atmosphere *(129)*.

129

BÉKÉSCSABA

"The world's largest village." The Slovak-Hungarian "population ex-change" after 1945 left its mark on the town. Even so, Békéscsaba re-mains the cultural center of Hungary's Slovak population. Its Slovak House is a late Classicist folk house from 1865 *(130)*.

GYULA

This brick castle was mentioned as early as 1405 *(131)*. Protected by a moat, it was built on a one-time flood area of the Fehér-Körös River. Gyula's cultural life is enriched by its Castle Theater.

130

131

HORTOBÁGY

Hortobágy National Park – in today's parlance – is a gene bank. What this means is the preservation of the old and the safeguarding of the new. The Hortobágy puszta, or Apaj puszta near Pest, or the Kiskunság National Park and others in Central Europe that, at the same time, offer something of a tourist site, showing part of the big Eurasian steppes. To preserve its rich flora and animals registered in the Red Book as endangered species. To

132

preserve the nesting place of the peculiar scooper (Recurvirostra avosetta), the lark (Calandrella brachydractyle), the affectedly aristocratic aigrette (Egretta alba) and the cranes (Grus grus) taking a rest on their several-thousand-kilometer-long round-trip journey and the several-thousand-strong flocks of the northern goose. And so many others. There needs to be one, two, three or even more places, vast and free, where the twisted-horn racka-sheep continues to be bred *(133)*, whose flocks are guarded by the black pumi or the white puli dogs *(132)*. Where the old Hungarian domestic animal species, not brought here (as mistakenly believed) by our ancestors from Asia, but valuable nonetheless, are not left on their own. And not only out of nostalgia. And not only scientifically. But for economic reasons as well. For if they are not valuable now, they could become valuable again later. Thus the puli, the pumi, the kuvasz and the komondor dogs, with their unique inherited features and developed over centuries of herding and guarding work, are once again bred for good money. The Hungarian

134

gray cattle *(134–135)* - an excellent draught animal thanks to its tremendous strength - was once taken to livestock markets across Europe. Although this beef is no longer prized by the market, it has been found to be of excellent nutritional value. It may perhaps become sought after again. Many visitors to Hortobágy are attracted here by the *fata morgana* caused by the light broken on the fronts of air mixing in various temperatures and density in the searing summer heat. Others are interested in the traces of the archaic herder's life. And the draw well. And the galloping stud *(136–137)*. The vast horizon. The romanticism of the puszta. That, hopefully, is not destroyed by the fact that Hortobágy is at once a precious museum and a living laboratory.

135

136

137

138

DEBRECEN

It is fitting to arrive at Debrecen, now Hungary's second most populous town, from Hortobágy, through the nine-arch bridge *(139)*. For Debrecen was kept alive for centuries by its agrarian environment – the once densely populated, then depopulated and deserted Hortobágy, providing a good pasture. Debrecen is a stubborn town. It is also referred to as the "Calvinist Rome." It soon took up the Helvetian faith, but remained closed to other strains of Protestantism such as Unitarism spreading from nearby Transylvania. In 1552 the Catholic religious services ceased here. Debrecen burghers, however, can count and bargain. Conclude a bargain and make a deal, if their interest so requires. Under the Turkish rule – after receiving numerous refugees and homeless – they lived through a number of ravages, paid much tax and tribute, but were never occupied. ts widely renowned institution, the Reformed College, has a past running straight back to 1538. From 1588, it has

139

been operating an academic faculty. It gained strength in 1660 when the Protestant professors and students of the nearby Nagyvárad – today Oradea in Romania – fled here. Its Classicist cathedral, which became a symbol of the town, was built in 1802, after the most severe of the fires that hit the town. The main facade wing of the College building *(140)* gained its present form then. Debrecen's lung is the long protected, yet repeatedly mutilated Nagyerdő (Big Forest) which, however, in its size and condition, is a good environment for the university and other institutions and for relaxation and making excursions. Every tree, shrub, grass and flower of its old oak park is under strict protection.

140

141

143

SZABOLCS–SZATMÁR–BEREG

Among the light string of the messages meant for the other world, a path of this world: All Soul's Day in a cool, rare mist upon sunset. The candle-light, reddish-gold shining of the cemeteries of tiny villages. While one fire wreath is left, the other one lights. Man planted settlements here, especially in the Tiszahát area and in the Szamos-Tisza corner. Or the Nyírség in springtime. Is it the visionary world of the writer Gyula Krúdy's pen? No, it is pure realism. The mist patches rise from the steaming soil at dawn here and swim man-high over the roads drawing witches and fairies – this is a real sight and not a dream. And from where we come and to where we go: water-mills, ancient churches with peasant wall

142

paintings, cemeteries with totems and wooden grave-posts –
and the apple orchards and acacia forests binding the soft
sand. The intersection of Slovakia, Ukraine and Hungary,
and, a bit farther south, of Ukraine, Romania and Hungary:
this is our East. These few pictures present only part of the
spectacle. Going to Csaroda, the botanist, the ecologist
searches for the moor-peat of the dead Tisza branches. Many
visit the folk historical monument Romanesque church,
which is a rare composition. Frescoes freed from under the
plaster from its Catholic era; there is wall painting in its nave,
unusual in a Protestant church (141). Its stuccoed wooden
ceiling is from 1777. The atmosphere of Nagykálló in the
Nyírség is not disturbed by the fashion of the end of this century: what the organic architecture fits into the environment
of old buildings really fits organically (142). The furnishing
of the ripe Gothic – today Reformed – church of
Nagyszekeres and the wooden bell tower are already
Baroque: What tradition the boat-shaped tomb-posts of
Szatmárcseke refer to is disputed (144); they are perhaps the
burials in boat coffins once customary (with the Vikings, for
example). They are now in a smaller, protected section of the
tomb-garden, where the ashes of the poet Ferenc Kölcsey,
the author of the Hungarian Hymn, rest. The naive-fantastic,
painted wooden tableaus of the Gothic church of Csen-
gersima, its interior transformed for Reformats after a plague
epidemic (145). The Reformed of Tákos carved wood,
plastered clay and painted their thick-set church colorfully
and decoratively at the end of the 1700s. Its bell tower (146),
as customary in this area, rises separately next to the church.

145

144

146

Budapest

*O*UR NEO-GOTHIC PARLIAMENT building looks over the Danube from Pest to Buda proudly, perhaps a little bit ostentatiously. It is the winner. Across from Parliament lies Buda's Castle Hill, fitted into the background of the Buda Hills. This was the first known human settlement in the area of today's capital: the *Homo erectus seu sapiens paleohungaricus* of Samuel's clan of Vértesszőlős inhabited its limestone caves several hundred thousand years ago. Then the focal point shifted toward the north. Legend holds – like the Hungarian legend of the magic deer – that the ancient Gauls, after fleeing from Troy and taking a long detour on their way west, stopped in Aquincum for several years. However, this – today's Óbuda – became Pannonia's main city. This place might have been the winter quarters of Attila, the grand prince of the Huns. After the Tartar devastation of 1241–42, when the royal center moved to Buda, onto Castle Hill, Óbuda was transferred to the queens. A castle was built for them, the ruins of which – unearthed and buried again – are hidden by the earth on the Danube quay. The ruling Turks also had their headquarters in the Buda Castle. After the Turks were chased out, the sound of the Hungarian language was long absent from the Left Bank of the Danube (Pest) under reconstruction. After a while, however, Pest provided an unquestionably better venue for launching industrial and economic development, the base of any modern metropolis. The name "Budapest" was used to describe the two towns as early as the beginning of the last century. But not until 1873, through the unification of Pest, Buda, Óbuda and Margaret Island, did Budapest become an actual, united city. In a capital that has gradually swelled to a city of two million inhabitants, the country's political and administrative center has increasingly shifted to the flat Pest side. This was the Pest Parliament's victory.

147

148

149

DOWNTOWN. Naturally, the heart of Pest. Citizens of Pest are themselves unsure where the borders of downtown lie. Strictly speaking, the area's southern section is bordered by the Danube and the Small Boulevard, and the northern area is the Lipótváros district. More broadly, downtown could be defined as what falls between the Danube and the Great Boulevard, which was once a branch of the Danube. But it certainly does not include the New Lipótváros, above the Margaret Bridge. The most widely

drawn borders for defining the downtown area are based on the density of the highest-class public buildings and apartment houses in the city. There is some basis for this, even if many of the structures – mainly the apartment houses – are fairly dilapidated today. One of the master-pieces of Hungarian Secession, the Museum of Applied Art, opened in 1896, represented – not only by its collection, but also by its interior and exterior – everything beautiful in architecture and handicrafts *(148)*. But surprisingly, a great number of apartment houses, like the one at Kossuth tér 13-15 near Parliament, were built with great artistic care. Almost excessively so, one might say today *(149)*. Budapest's Catholic cathedral, the Saint Stephen Basilica *(150–151)* was built with great care between 1848–1905.

150

151

It is only out of tradition that the one-row streets along
the Danube river embankment in Pest and Buda are called
quays: they have not been that for long. The Belgrád quay –
its upper section between the Elizabeth Bridge and the
Chain Bridge – is actually the Danube promenade. In earlier
times, it belonged to the people of Pest. Nowadays it belongs
instead to foreign visitors staying in one of the many-star
hotels towering above the place. They are the ones who can

152

153

154

see the elegant Széchenyi Chain Bridge *(152)*, the stone latticework of the Fishermen's Bastion on the Buda Castle Hill in front, the one-time Royal Palace – today a museum complex – and the glittering mirror windows of Hotel Hilton *(154)* raised on the ruins of a Dominican cloister. And it is they who help us notice, in the increasingly dense jungle of sights in the Hungarian capital, what has been preserved beautifully or what has remained beautiful on its own. They stop and look up onto the mosaic on the facade of the building at Szervita tér 3 depicting the apotheosis of Hungária *(153)*. They admire, the twin Klotild palaces, one of which stands in front of Kossuth Lajos utca *(156)* so that the huge traffic through the Elizabeth Bridge is forced to take a slight detour at its foot. And visitors may discover the oriental facade *(155)* a minute's walk away, Károly körút.

155

156

157

160

BIRD'S-EYE VIEW. It is said that, at the completion of the Museum of Applied Art *(157)* – with all its adornments (or perhaps at the completion of the Geological Institute) *(158)*, Ödön Lechner – the leading architect of the Hungarian Secessionist school – was asked: Why put the most careful touches on the roof, even sections too high to be seen by passersby? "Because birds can see it," the Master allegedly replied. Let's not mention the fact that the writer Victor Hugo said something similar concerning the Paris Notre Dame, because there the builder referred not to birds but to God, justifiably so for a church. Since then, aviation has become an everyday occurrence. And man, after God and birds, discovered in a novel way how spectacular the town sections, buildings or square compositions are from above. Two examples: the majestic Opera House built by Miklós Ybl on Andrássy út *(160)*, and Heroes' Square (Hősök tere) with the Millennium Memorial with its grim-looking sculptures *(151)* and with the Museum of Fine Arts *(152)*.

161

162

91

BRIDGES. Each has its history. Each has its character. None escaped the devastation of World War II. Their redesigning and rebuilding took place according to different principles. The Szabadság (Freedom) Bridge, built in 1896 and faithfully restored in 1946 *(163)*, can no longer bear the heavy mass-transport use. Margaret Bridge, serving the Margaret Island since 1876 *(164)* did not change much during its reconstruction in 1947–1948. Four lions, two at each entrance, guard the Chain Bridge, the first permanent bridge over the Danube in Budapest, built between 1839 and 1849; 100 years after

163

164

165

its first inauguration, the bridge, recreated as faithfully as possible and partly from its old steel plates, was opened to traffic again *(166–167)*. And to the admiring eye. To replace the original Elizabeth Bridge, which opened in 1903, a slender, elegant cable bridge *(164, 168)* with an entirely new shape was inaugurated in 1964.

166

167

168

169

BATHS. Unlike any other capital city in the world, Budapest – thanks to its limestone foundations and the spring and thermal waters working their way to the surface – is a city of caves and baths at the same time. Witnessed by the ruins of the city of Aquincum *(169)*, members of the legions serving here and the Romanized citizens of Pannonia alike took advantage of the spring waters gushing up in Buda. And most architectural relics that remained from the Turkish occupation are djamis, minarets – and baths. Among these is today's Király-fürdő *(170)*, whose bath hall from the Turkish era was completed later by Baroque and Classicist sections.

170

MARGARET ISLAND. Its ancient small fortresses guarded important Danube crossing points in the Roman era. It was a royal quarter in the Middle Ages. Primarily, however, cloisters were built on this 100-hectare island lying between the two branches of the Danube. Only ruins remained of the Dominican, Premontrean and Franciscan cloisters. What is regarded today as the Premontrean chapel *(171)* was built in this century, by incorporating the remnants and the stones of the ruined cloister's church. The island's name comes from King Béla IV's daughter, Margaret, a Dominican nun, whom his father, after escaping from the Tartars' ravage, offered her as Christ's virgin in an oath he swore. And the girl, who later became Saint Margaret of the Arpad Dynasty, took this so seriously that her royal father, who later changed his mind, tried in vain to marry her off. Today most of Margaret Island is a magnificent park *(172)*. There are several sports facilities, an open-air theater and two hotels based on excellent curative water on the island.

171

172

GELLÉRT HILL. Sacrificial stones provide evidence that, long ago, a Celtic-Roman cult center stood on top of the hill. Who knows whether that has any connection with the fact that pious Christians later labeled it the place where evil witches gathered at night. Or is it the traces of the story of the martyr Saint Gellért? Gellért of Venice, on his way to the Holy Land, was kept in Hungary by King Stephen *(173)* as his son's teacher. Pagans in revolt roped Gellért on a coach and sent him to martyrdom, pushing him off what was then called Kelen hill, now bearing Gellért's name. His sculpted hand with the cross rises to bless the city – or perhaps to prove that he became stronger in his death *(174)*.

173

174

Toward Castle Hill. Approaching it from
any direction, one can reach Castle Hill through
narrow streets around its base, leading to snaking
detours or stairways.

That is, as long as one is not stopped by some
especially romantic detail *(176)* or building, such
as the one-time White Cross Inn *(175)* on Batthyány tér.
The passing of time has lifted the street level before it,
as if it had been sunk in a small pit.

It is widely believed that the peculiar figure of European
Enlightenment, Joseph II, emperor of Austria and king
of Hungary, once stayed in this gracious Rococo
building for a few days.

He never had himself crowned. And he avoided
the royal palace. On a more risqué historical note,
the uncrowned king of womanizing, Giovanni Giacomo
Casanova, was also a guest of the house.

175

176

In The Buda Castle. Excavations reveal that here on Castle Hill the royal residence was originally farther north; it was later settled on the southern edge of the heights above the Danube. It was rebuilt again and again after the devastation of armies, and after changes in taste. Thus the royal palace (almost entirely destroyed in the last siege in 1944–1945) was designed in a Neo-Baroque style in the postwar reconstruction. After long hesitation and disputes over whether the palace section of the Castle – renovated in prolonged, costly steps *(178, 180)* – should be a presidential residence and a governmental center again as before or a cultural

177

179

178

center, the latter viewpoint won out. Thus the Budapest Museum and the Recent History Museum, the Hungarian National Gallery and the National Széchényi Library are housed in the palace's main wings. The man who beat the Turks, Eugene of Savoy, is memorialized by a mounted sculpture in front of the palace's eastern facade (177–178, 180). Lajos Petri's Hussar Memorial on one of the western bastions of the Castle (179). "The Cowboy" by György Vastagh Jr. does not ride proudly, but breaks in his still unbroken horse; the placement of the sculpture here comes as no surprise for those who are aware that the palace's riding arena once stood here. The turul (181), the bird of prey flying over the pusztas of ancient Hungarians, is a column decoration. No ornithologist can identify its species, for it is a mythical animal, a protective totem bird.

180

181

182

184

At a glance it appears that the Matthias Church and the Fishermen's Bastion *(183)* in the Buda Castle are of the same age, made by the same hand. Which is a little bit true and very much untrue. If one takes a closer view of the latter *(184–185)*, he'll become suspicious. The history of the Gothic Matthias (or rather Our Lady's) Church boasts a long history from its Romanesque core (which already showed its present form) to rebuilding and reshaping in the Gothic style, to the restoration of its collapsed southern tower by King Matthias (who thus became the eponym of the church), to its Baroque transformation according to the Jesuit taste, to the reconstruction of the church under the guidance of Frigyes Schulek, the leading master of Hungarian late Eclecticism between 1874 and 1896. Posterity records this work with great esteem but with reservations about its principles. By the time it was completed, the deteriorated state of the shining church's eastern side on the Danube front was noticed. Then, Frigyes Schulek built the flashy, many-towered Fishermen's Bastion – fittingly, described as Romanesque. Like it or not, the century in between has made it a historical monument. Today it is perhaps the most frequently photographed object in the capital. Its pit holds the Saint Stephen Memorial *(185)* by the sculptor Alajos Stróbl, with its pedestal designed by Schulek.

185

83

101

A strange mix of towers: a glance from the Neo-Gothic, brick Reformed Church situated on Szilágyi Dezső tér in Buda and on the Hotel Matthias Rex house of the Hilton hotel chain behind, with the tower of the one-time Saint Nicholas Church incorporated into the hotel complex *(186)*. The corner balcony of the old Buda Town Hall looking onto Szentháromság tér; the sculpture of town-protecting Pallas Athene before it *(187)*. The ruins of the Mary Magdalene church in Kapisztrán tér, which faced the wrecking ball after irreparable damage in World War II, with one of its tracery windows reconstructed by memory *(188)*. Tárnok

187

186

188

utca 14: a 14th-century Gothic apartment house, with a protruding story from the 15th century. The protruding section was later walled under; its original shape and its medieval geometric painting was uncovered only by the devastation in 1944–1945 *(189)*. The elegantly winding Úri utca. From the right, the primate's palace with wrought iron balcony bars in the Zopf style *(191)*. Considering the traffic in the Castle district, the flocks of visitors who need to be served and even the harmonization of the old buildings with the new ones *(190)*, one can see that it is difficult to be a world heritage. But that has been said before...

189

190

191

192

PRINTED IN HUNGARY, 1998
Printed in KNER NYOMDA RT. DÜRER NYOMDA AND KIADÓ KFT, GYULA
ISBN 963 548 338 4